About the Author

Dominick Nicotra is one of 7 siblings who grew up in Brooklyn, New York. My mother was my biggest inspiration.

I am a 52 year old gay man. I came out of the "closet" when I was 19. Even though I was 19 when I came out, I knew all along of my true self.

My writing's started when I was in my late teenage years. I would walk through Manhattan, but unlike most, I would observe people. I enjoy Life, and the many people who visit, or reside in New York.

My first poem was inspired by numerous faces encountered, as I aimlessly walked the city for hours; I have observed many different people from many different walks of life.

I write to inspire, and educate people. Darkness may fall but there is always light at the end of the tunnel. Clouds appear in many different shades of darkness, in everyone's life from time to time, but the sun is always more powerful than the darkest cloud, and the sun will always shine through. My poetry is written to relate to all situations in life.

Special Acknowledgements: Thank you to my sister, **Lisa Nicotra**, a close friend **Dr. Richard Maggio** and, my Therapist and close friend **Keith McFall** , as they all encouraged me to pursue my dream to write this book, providing me with their honest input, and continuous support and love.

I was a confident teenager that still possessed the innocence, vulnerability, and I must say I was a bit naïve. The many different people I observed while I strolled through the Manhattan, New York City streets, it was an eye opener, as well as an inspiration for this poem. This is also the very first poem I wrote.

Visions of sadness and inspiration

Different colors, different ways
Hearts on fire like a blaze
They pass on by with a smile,
But don't expect them to go the extra mile
They all carry beauty in their own little way
They're all self conscience of what people might say
They hide themselves from the world they live in finding
themselves in a bar, drowning their sorrows in a bottle
of gin why would be go through such extremes? Could it
be their secrets, dreams, or silent screams?
You might ask yourself who these people may be
It's people with problems that others can't see

CHAPTER 1

FAITH

Friends

Don't go, stay

A reversal of who I use to be,
Nonexistent draped under a canopy

Who is this stranger in the reflection,
Scorned, beaten, with plenty of rejection

A Leper hidden from society,
diminishing of someone's vitality

Staring at a clock as the time goes by slowly,
Will religion fulfill the loneliness, turning everything holy ?

A touch, a caress as one yearns for some affection,
A bulge in a pair of jeans, fantasizing of a mouth injection

The mind scrambles, as the voice inside says "this life is not familiar",
The heart screams where did you go, your behavior is peculiar.

To go or not to go remains the question,
As tears pour out of the eyes with no hesitation.

Everything one wants becomes unreachable,
A new way of life, as the ignorant are untouchable

A new friend came along and provided outstanding guidance,
A subject filled with negativity and reluctance

Months pass by, a new outlook took form,
Like a student studying profusely, and ready to step out of the dorm

All that was gone found its way back,
As the sun shines brightly eliminating the black.

The beat of a drum inside of a chest,
The eyes close at night with plenty of rest.

From the first time meeting this brilliant, sexy, caring guy, he stated " don't go,
stay",
Suicide is not the answer, I am here to remold you into something beautiful,
from a mound of clay.

I love, live, and established a new set of goals,
I adore this man, for he held all the controls

AND SO I KEPT LIVING.

Suicide is not the answer

The days when you want to say goodbye
When life is tough and you want to die
Look deep inside your soul
Grab my hand, I will lift you out of that hole
Giving up is not a resolution
Even though one might think it's a simple solution
Problems come and go
As you learn you will grow
Release your tears and screams
Establish a goal and a new set of dreams
Even when you feel no one is there
Look around and you will find many who do care

This poem is for suicide awareness. I have been there and so have many others

Self Love Exposed

Feelings hidden behind a wall
Securing a place ensuring not to fall
Emotions trapped at the bottom of the sea
Keeping the mind clear of what could be
The need for love and compassion
Ran out like a fad in fashion
Fantasies swim up- stream
Occurring while sleeping and kept in a dream
The waking moment to focus on me
As an inner love surfaced the captives were set free

The achievable wall

It was a big wall
withstanding all sorts of weather, as it stood tall
A greatness of materials made from nature
A climb not suited for every creature
Only the determined would attempt to climb it
Different body types from the muscular to the not so fit
This wall does not discriminate
To fail it would eliminate
A day has come for the attempt
A struggle that left oneself in contempt
Ambitious to get up and over the wall
The climb was a challenge as one is careful not to fall
Reaching the top in victory
As you make it over, you forget your history
The wall is a real life game
Starting from the bottom and not so tame
Courage and strength is your friend
It will help you achieve it, up until the end
As long as you give it your all
What was once intimidating is now the achievable wall

I am Ready

The light in the eyes
A smile with no disguise
Outlook ready to shine
Claiming all that's mine
Moving forward with a clean slate
With a mind in a healthy state
A fire raging inside
Getting ready for the ride
With a future unclear
Giving faith and fate the wheel to steer

I am ready!

A stir of echo's

Each day I awake to a new man in my bed
a reflection in the mirror stirring various thoughts in my head

The face, skin, and body are the same
Realization in the brain saying it's not your frame

Years of yearning for a dim light
Darkness covered more than the night

Echoes of the inner voice wanting to be heard
Waiting for a listening ear to hear every word

A stranger would be the key to change
Brightness and happiness in a heightened range

The teachings he provided would sculpt a new me
the various men in my bed were finally set free

And the wall collapsed

The serenity of the rain
as memories stimulate the brain
a picture speaks in silence
flashbacks of the violence
triggering different feelings
like bees swarming as one stings
the years have passed, I'm a new me
the struggle to survive was the key
a Battle between letting down my wall
protecting all of me so I don't fall
inner strength now exist
the coldness allows to resist
misunderstood by harshness
always distributing kindness
The day will come when the bricks will fall
I'll have the control of the destruction of the wall

Inner peace

Quiet the mind with a favorite song,
Hold back your emotions, and sing strong
A kind word spoken to a reflection in the mirror,
Control your thinking for you are not inferior
A stroll in the night will relieve the stress,
The longer the walk, the negative thoughts will digress
What was or what could've been are an illusion ,
Focusing on the present without confusion
To love yourself is a necessity ,
Take pride for who you are, as the soul lives in tranquility
A shadow seen in the sun is the only darkness one should witness
A new state has taken form, a healthy chore called inner fitness

Hear Me

Listen to my words
Listen with your eyes
Listen to my body language
without judgment and despise

Hear with your ears
See with your sight
I am human with feelings
Please don't put up a fight

Embrace me with your love
Guide me with your light
I will do the same as we both take flight

Hear me with every inch of my being
as we celebrate without grieving

Hear me!

Gravitation

He cuddled each night with his fears
Falling asleep with eyes full of tears
To the world he wore a smile
With a heart willing to go the extra mile
Deep wounds and scars were hidden below layers of the skin
The hurt was disguised by a big grin
Coming to terms with all the major issues
Would involve opening up and a few boxes of tissues
To expel all the ill feelings that exist
An open heart and mind is required and both won't resist
The body rid of all the negativity
He is now grounded not only by gravity

CHAPTER 2

FATE

FATE

The stars they shine so bright
flickering like a candle
Illuminating the sky with its beauty
On a clear day it gives the illusion of closeness
Reaching a hand upwards in hopes to touch it
Gazing for hours in a tranquil state
Wishing upon a star in hopes to determine ones fate

Yesteryear

A flower, a picture, a voice, a song, or a scent
striking a memory in the brain, like a permanent dent

A touch, a smile, or the color of someone's eyes
can bring back a time one would like to reprise

A Street; a name; or even a game
reliving a flashback of an old flame

As the years pass by the memories stay alive
the pleasant memories, one should not deprive

Wanting to feel the happiness that once was near
with no fear leaving those memories in the yesteryear

The Reason

The tears I shed
As the heart bled
A smile that faded
Left him jaded
All the things that a relationship was to be
Were imaginary and washed out to sea
Left stigmatized by your selfishness
While all along the other showed selflessness
In pursuit of something real
What I have to offer others won't deal
I often wonder if this is a bad dream
To lie in bed as you want to scream
Strength comes from your inner self
Learning to keep all of what you feel on a shelf
No one will ever understand my mind
It's easier to ignore and leave behind
As we approach another season
Still no answer as to what was the reason

In life you live and learn
consequences will leave you to burn

Goals versus Dreams

The words flow like a stream
a night and shining armor in a dream
reality versus fantasy is life a figment of our imagination?
or is everything a real creation?
The Soul soars at night
always ready to take flight
Destination goal is to reach a shining star
getting past the mountains, it seems so far
choices to be happy or sad
values making "one" good or bad
This rollercoaster we ride each day
determines our final destination as a permanent stay.

Ruins from a Tornado

Destroying a life in the midst of a storm
as the tornado entered, the ruins would take form
Not prepared for the aftermath
All was blurry, leaving no path
The inner hate had to settle a score
This wasn't what I signed up for
Living a life with all the repercussions
A couch a therapist, and many discussions
The purity that existed was stolen away
Unable to trust, is that why a new love won't stay?
The tears flow but yet unseen
A black heart that needs to be washed clean
Years have passed and the scars still exist
A new me formed after I tried to resist
Learning to love yourself again was the plan
Leaving the past in its own time span
inner strength and faith is what got me through
The heart bloomed with love as ambitions grew
The thought that such dark evil roams the earth
Placed many walls and a rebirth

The Gift

Given something by surprise
Eyes swelled up, it was something to despise
Years of living a protected life
This "gift" was similar to a heart stabbed with a knife
The never ending tears
As you're facing your worst fears
A lifetime sentence given as your sent to prison
Permanent life changes have arisen
The devil played you good without a warning
The brain is in continuous mourning
Restricted with all aspects of normality
Keeping the "gift" in check is just a formality
Acceptance has become a quest
Keeping your composure as you try to look your best
No one knows what it's like to accept such a "gift"
Until it happens to them, they will never get your drift
Numbness with no feeling
This "gift" given is the "gift" of stealing
Channeling into your spirituality
The need for healing has become a reality
"Gifts" can be good or bad
They can make you happy or sad
Anyone can receive a surprise
Just be "careful" it's not the devil in disguise

Tears of a clown

A mask covering a face
Tears hidden without a trace
a painted on smile to hide all the pain
Showering sunshine during the downpour of rain
Funny jokes were an escape
afraid reality would start to drape
nobody would ever see him down
behind the façade laid the tears of a clown

Take my hand

Walk with me as You take my hand
I will lead you on a path, I promise that is grand
A world where demons don't exist
A private party of two, how could you resist
Nights of cuddling and filled with love
Two lives intertwined like a fitted glove
Take my hand with no regret
I'll tear down that wall with no fret
We will build a paradise for all to see
Love disbursed with no controversy
Take my hand we will guide each other
as we build a world for both of us to discover

Take my hand .....

The "Key"

You will see me hurt but never see my tears
You will see my accomplishments but not my fears
You will see my love but never see hate
You will see my faith flourish as it determines my fate
You will see my inner beauty as it covers my outer exterior
You will see I will never consider you as an inferior
You will see me for the person that I am
You will see I am courageous as a lion and calm as a lamb
You will see all the things I have stated
No fakeness or being baited

I am me for all to see
As you break down my wall the reward will be a "key"

Faith and Fate

Years of dating and a couple of lovers
Hearts race in the beginning, until it uncovers.
Familiarity starts to play a major role,
Feelings change as words take control.
Fifty-fifty doesn't exist,
One is more selfish as they persist.
I love you are three words constantly misused,
Leaves the heart and mind very confused.
As you continue to seek out love from different faces,
Men hide their feelings and leave no traces.
A lifestyle difficult to live,
Scars from the past that you try to forgive.
Leaving one isolated in a single status,
This guy thinks with his brain and not his apparatus.
One day I will meet my soul mate,
Until then I will rely on faith and fate.

Who we are

Who are you?
A person of flesh and bones, known by few
Left behind were many he outgrew

Who are you?
One who hurts behind his smile
yet, someone who still goes the extra mile?

Who are you?
Someone who leads a lifestyle that still discriminate

Hate exists in this world, refusing to be incriminated

Who are you?
A grown man who has experienced the good with the bad
Staying optimistic, leaving pessimism like it's a fad.

Who are you?
A man who places his family and close friends first
A heart full of love, a significant other can quench his thirst

I am,
Everything that life has taught me through the storms
As we grow a new person forms

Perfection

What is perfection?
An interpretation or perception?
How one displays their heart and soul?
High expectations, achievements, or a set goal
a form of a body defined as skinny, muscular or full figured
a calm mind, or one that is constantly triggered?
Various eye colors that would attract one to read
Selflessness, or a person full of greed?
The tone of a voice ranging from a high pitch to low
Different smiles as feelings start to grow
the moral of this poem is that we are unique and perfect in our own
way
it's the uniqueness of each and everyone of us that brings light to
every new day

Secret confessions

The heart wants to confess
Love hides behind a wall in distress
Feelings are sacred within the soul
Everything that was felt in the past, you stole
Thoughts scramble in the mind
Concentration is hard to find
Yearning to feel your touch
Reciprocation would never be too much
The eyes seek for your smile
The lips kiss yours in a hot passionate style
A tale of secret confessions
An imagery of both of our reflections

Apologies

Apologies come in all forms
Quite often through many storms
Some are silent and shown with a gesture
As others sit quietly and make it fester
A gift as a token of a resolution
Setting the issue into its own institution
A silent apology with tears in the eyes
Says the heart is sorry with no disguise
Sex is a way to eliminate the hate
A few hours of pleasure to restrain it behind a gate
A kiss on the cheek wrapped with a big hug
Quietly lying together on a bear rug
As you see there are many ways to apologize
Setting the anger free leading the heart and mind to compromise

CHAPTER 3

LOVE

Spirit of Mom

I look up to the sky and see your face
memories of your beauty and your grace
The day you left my heart shattered
Tears fell from my eyes, and a mind was battered
I often wonder how you are, as you sweep through the skies,
guiding me with your light to ensure everlasting ties
The bond between a mother and son lasts forever
I will know that you are around each time I find a feather
one day our worlds will once again collide
until then, I will continue to enjoy life, or as we call it this "ride"

Big Brother

Dedicated to my Brother Eugene (a bind for eternity)

The yesteryears remain in the heart and mind
Precious moments taken for granted, bound and bind
Jokes, smiles, and stories shared
An ending that was never thought of, but was feared
Ashes placed in the ground
As the heart cries, no words are found
Days go by as we try to move on
Memories remain as the physical appearance is gone
A bond for eternity that could never be broken
The love trapped inside kept as a token
A brother, a friend, that will last forever
Memories of you, I will always treasure

Season's change

Like all four seasons, everyone's life can relate
We meet people through different stages, some leave and some escalate
Feelings of love, set the stage
Emotions grow, and some disintegrate into rage
Season's are repeated with new faces
Learning and lessons set the path with new spaces
Expectations should not play a role
It can leave a heart that has taken its toll
A fresh outlook with a new season approaching
The mind provides the heart with plenty of coaching
Leaving the past where it belongs
As the heart will play new songs
Challenges occur and are a part of life
If you choose to challenge someone's heart, it will cut you like a knife
Let love happen with its natural state
As two hearts live in sync with no debate
We all have different goals set
Regardless of what aspect of your life, don't ever regret
A mixture of determination, faith and love , peak at a different range
As you smile and walk forward without fear, that's when you will know when the season's change

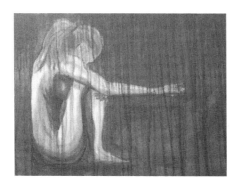

The yearning

Look into the soul of my eyes, what do you see?
Lay your head on my chest, hear the heartbeat as feelings flow free
Hold my hand, as we stroll down the street,
For we are the only two who exist, with no one to defeat
Speak in a monotone voice, even when tensions run high
Communication is the key, avoiding both to cry
Gestures with a smile, makes one look seductive
Enough for a partner succumb to being inductive
Lay with me as you promise to never leave
A commitment as we grow old together, two lives will never grieve
The book has started with chapter one
With many more pages to fill until the book is done

..........A never ending story

My Only Desire

Funny, sexy, strong, grounded, and kind hearted
Open to love and unguarded
Breaking through walls with understanding
Sharing two lives without being demanding
Is this a fantasy sought? or does it exist?
Are you someone that would give in and not resist?
So many yearn for what is stated
As they act out differently from being jaded
Continuing to search for a soul that's on fire
Once the soul mates meet, you will be the only desire

Single Status

Years of dating and a couple of lovers
Hearts race in the beginning until it uncovers
Familiarity starts to play a major role
Feelings change as words get out of control
Fifty- fifty doesn't exist
One is more selfish as they persist
I love you are three words misused
Leaves the heart and mind confused
As you continue to seek out love from different faces
Men hide their feelings as they leave no traces
A lifestyle so hard to live
Scars from the past that you try and forgive
Leaving one isolated in a single status
This guy thinks with his brain and not his apparatus
One day I will meet my soul-mate

Until then I will rely on faith and fate

My true love

The heart still carries a memory
Our bodies were in harmony
Lying awake while he slept
Staring for hours was a secret well kept
His soul shined through his beautiful eyes
No flaws found that I could despise
Spontaneous and sexy is a good descriptive
His feelings were hidden but yet so sensitive
The excitement of watching him shower
He was the total package who held all the power
The day came when we would part
I was ready to expose my love but he already made a new start
Choosing to keep the heart safe and secure
A wall was built as well as the development of a new flaw
Till this day he remains "my true love"
No one has ever measured up so I could never rise above
Tears that once shed
A heart that once bled
Came to an end with an optimistic view
If I would've spoken up, our love would have grew
My heart sang, but my mouth stood silent
His ears didn't hear the commitment
The mind, heart, and voice are all in sync
My next true love will never have to think

Dream Lover

My dream lover is out there
Come seek me out, if you dare
Empowered by a connection
Seeking more than just a superficial reflection
Why are you hiding ? Come take a stand
Tell me your inner most secrets, as we walk hand and hand
You will already know me from the look in my eyes
As feelings are drawn outwards, with no disguise
I know who you are, I see you in my dreams
Whenever we meet, I awake as the sunlight beams
We are connected already threw the powers of the universe
As I wait, more poems will disburse

Synergy

Being dominant but yet submissive
Surrendering your body and soul to be permissive
Mysterious and intensive eyes
We lock into each other with no disguise
A love buried deep within
Happiness is seeing a grin
Never underestimate the power of energy
As two bodies collide in synergy

Insync

To love with no return
Brings the heart to the knees
Years of searching
Kind of like withered trees
will the heart find what its yearning
Or will it be declared for the embodiment of oneself?
Fate and future is by determination
following through will lead to an accomplishment
the powerful heart and mind
once in sync a true love one will find

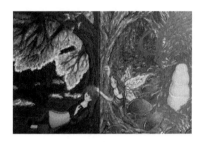

Fantasy or Reality

His eyes spoke to me
Emotions swam like fishes in the sea

Lost in a trance with a simple glance
playing it cool in a subtle stance

The mind playing off of a certain gesture
wanting to know his every pleasure

The hand needing to caress his face
As the beating heart starts to race

Sexiness within his smile
A body dressed in a fierce style

This fantasy man made of all that's desired
or is he a reality and nothing has transpired

As I end my first book of poetry, I would like to thank each and every one of you for taking the time to read, feel, and diagnose your own interpretation of each poem written.

"it's easier to act out our nightmares, it's when we step out of the darkness and start achieving our dreams, that's when we start living" my own quote

Light, love and peace to all !

Made in the USA
Columbia, SC
17 May 2021